This book contains cussin' 'n shit.

First published in the United States 2016
by The Rayloc Group
Ingelwood, CA
1 2 3 4 5 6 7 8 9 10
Miss Innocent Goes to Kool Skool and Other Silly Stuff/ by Michael Colyar;
illustrated by Ivan Artucovich
edited by Sharai Robbin
layout & design by Good Ground Literary Services

Summary: A collection of contemporary poetry by legendary comedian, Michael Colyar.

ISBN 978-0-692-77311-6

Miss Innocent Goes to Kool Skool and Other Silly Stuff

A Poetry Book for ADULT Children

Michael Colyar

GOD IS EVERYTHING!

Table of Contents

Forward
by
Les Brown

I have been fortunate to meet many talented and gifted people. Two, who stand out most in my mind for their ability to change peoples' lives with the power of the written word, are Maya Angelou and Michael Colyar.

You are in for a treat. Get ready to meet someone that you thought you already knew. We have known him as a comedian and now, with this life transforming work as a poet, he takes us on a roller coaster ride of life which will make you laugh, talk to yourself and scream with tears of joy.

The first time I heard these words read to me by Michael Colyar in my hotel room, I sat captivated, mesmerized by the spirit expressed through his words that touched me deep inside. This is a book you want to curl up in bed with, shut out the world, create a space without any interruptions, so that you can savor each moment.

Several times I closed my eyes and fought back tears that were provoked by the beauty, elegance, and sheer passion that radiated from each poem. Like two little boys, we laughed and high-fived, acknowledging that God took over this writing project, showing up and showing out. Michael C and this collection of thoughts, feelings, and reflections of life will come to be known as healing balm for the soul.

If you ever sat in the audience and experienced his humor, you would know, without question that Michael has something special. This higher calling on his life and his mother's prayers liberated him from the jaws of death and made it possible for him to bless us with this writing project. Out of the bowels of his pain, he found the strength to make us laugh, becoming known as the "King of Venice Beach". Now, we get an opportunity to go into his mind, see through his eyes and benefit from his insights and view of life.

Michael's thoughts, words, and feelings, conveyed through this work, will transform your mind, touch your heart and penetrate your soul. This is a book for grown-up children that speaks to the child in all of us and reconnects us with part of ourselves that many of us had forgotten through the experience of life. Each page will trigger something inside of you that will make you "remember when." It will make you laugh, make you cry, and motivate you to love and live at a deeper level.

It has been said that passion is God's will in us. This book is written from that place. Michael, thank you for allowing God to use you as an instrument to produce this creative work. I am sure your mother is looking from heaven with my mother saying, "That's my boy. He has made me proud again."

Les Brown
Author: "Live Your Dreams", "It's Not Over 'til You Win", "In Pursuit of Greatness"
Motivational Speaker and Speaker Coach

Dedication

I dedicate this poetry book to three of the greatest people in my life:

Marylena Smith, who was Marylena Colyar before that and Marylena Pratt before that, but always her own person and always an awesome mother who gave her all for us, and even after transcending, she is still giving to my brothers and me. If she only had $10.00 she would spend $9.99 on us without a doubt or hesitation. Oh, some would say, "She's supposed to. She's your Mom". And altho' that thought is true, there are a lot of moms that would only go 50/50. Lol. She is one of my greatest heroes and my best friend ever...and she still is.

Kellie Antoinette McCann, for loving me, inspiring me, teaching me, encouraging me, saving me, healing me, freeing me, and for saying "yes" when I asked her to be mine for life, be my wife, and to keep our light of love, passion, and God lit and shining for the world to see. She is beautiful, for sure, but her vibrant spirit kicks out a light of joy that dims all beauty in comparison. Or maybe I just feel that way because I love her so. May we be an example that love changes you and makes you better and better and better... or at least happier and happier and happier.

And...

To my Godfather, teacher, friend, and all around amazing man, Dan Enright, who believed in me first in Hollywood and took real chances for me. This little old Jewish guy who, at 65 years old, was riding his bike on Venice Beach one day and caught my performance and believed in me so much he put me on my first national TV show, then he put me in a movie I was terrible in, it was called "Necessity" starring Loni Anderson, and I stunk and he still loved me. He helped me raise my son and bought him his first bike, he kept encouraging me and invited me and my ex to get married at his home and he never wanted anything from me. I used to tell everybody he was my Godfather – 'cause he was surely a father figure to me, a mentor, a mensch - and he would always say, "I don't want to be your father, I am your brother. I am your friend." I love you, man. I just hope you like how I turned out. Namaste

heroes and my best friend Ever....and she still is.

Acknowledgments

I thank Brooks, my ex-wife, for traveling most of the early journey with me. A big shout out to Ms. September Pierce: a woman small in physical stature but large of heart. Thanks for helping keep it moving.

I surely wouldn't be whoever I am today without growing up with my fantastic, eclectic, brilliant, crazy, fly and, in their own personal ways, magical brothers: David Jr., Yoland, Ronald and Courtney. All are different in their own beautifully strange ways and I love them all with all my heart.

Though scarcely mentioned here, there was a guy who made that all possible for my entire family, my father, David Lee Colyar - haberdasher, gentleman and truly great father who left this planet when I was only 12, which limits my access, but doesn't diminish my love and gratitude to him. He was a fantastic father. Everybody loved him.

My mother, Marylena Smith, insisted that we know words. If you didn't know a word she'd make you look it up. You would have to be able to spell it, pronounce it, and give its definition. I have made a bunch of money in this life because of my fabulous command of the English language...words.

I acknowledge my mom because she gave me the tools necessary to be a comedian, actor, writer, director, motivational speaker, producer, teacher, poet, rapper, and now author (which is really just a fancy word for writer...okay, so I'm double dippin'). She gave me the tools to have a great life.

The best thing we can be as adults is good parents. My mom was one and my father wasn't too shabby, either.

I love you, momma and I'm glad you got the chance to see Barack Obama come on in. Most of all...I acknowledge God who makes all things possible. Everything is about family and God. Once you get family and God down everything else takes care of itself.

Introduction

Miss Innocent Goes to Kool Skool…and Other Silly Stuff (A Poetry Book for Adult Children)

This is the writer's attempt at explanation through semi-formal introduction… but basically, you're on your own.

Someone asked, "What are adult children?" Oh, that's simple; any adult who still embraces and dances in the light of their youth. You know…you all growed up and errthing but still like sailing through the adventures of life with your inner child still screaming and cussin', hollerin', and fussin' in the spirit of the ageless free.   Still too heavy? Okay. Let's try this; big folks who still like being a kid… sometimes. Lol.

Initial Statement: The title of the book has absolutely nothing to do with its contents. The title was inspired by my ex-wife, Brooksie, who when I met her 24 years ago, was as naïve as a newborn pup. Now after a fifth of a century of hanging out with riffraff like me, she has matured into not only a cool character, but at times, she's downright hip…and knows her way around the block. The poems in this book for "adult children" were written over a period of 20 years. They speak to various parts and times and experiences of my life; my challenges and my triumphs, my wild successes and my silly failures, things that made me laugh and a few that still bring the occasional tear. All of it I honor.

Remember kids, bless everything, because everything that ever happened to you brought you to this day, this moment, this book. The poems were designed with you in mind. Yeah, you, my brothers and sisters, no matter what form or shade you seem to assume, I love you all, for I can only find myself in the mirror image of you.

Closing Statement: Having said all that, please disregard the Initial Statement. P.S. If you don't like my book, please don't tell nobody. I need the money bad…I'm trying to get my car fixed.

Pax,
Michael

February 9,2016
Ain't Life Grand?

You Can't Have Me

You can take my house-take my home
Take all the things you think I own
You may take away my flesh and bone
But, you can't have me

You can take away my lovely bed
Take away the meat and bread
You can rip these eyes out of my head
But, you can't have me

For now my vision is totally clear
And in my heart there is no fear
For now I know that God is here
And you can't have me

Do let's end this external war
My tender heart is worn and sore
And I will love you ever more
But, you
        Cant
            Have
                Moi

Fly
Dedicated to Everyone

Seems funny while I'm browsing
Or reading through a book
That I hear this buzz buzz buzzing
And I have to stop and look

At first I don't see anything
Then this motion hits my eye
It's that nasty filthy creature
We disgustingly call a fly

Well, he'll buzz it here and buzz it there
And zoom right past your face
Then you look around for something
That you hope can stop his pace

But you must not move too quickly
As you plan to make your play
Or that slimy little parasite
Will simply fly away

Then you see this little magazine
You know will do the trick
So you pick it up real slowly
But you've got to swing it quick

Or that bloody little bugger's
Gonna bug you all night long
As he whistles and he twistles
And he sings his buggy song

He'll sing buzzy buzzy boo boo
And buzzy buzzy beer
As he buzzes past your midnight snack
And he buzzes past your ear

As he buzzes past your ham and cheese
And buzzes past your pie
As he lands upon your radio
Now you've got him in your eye

So you stand up slowly, slowly now
You must not blow your chance
To smash this creepy little fly
And end his hectic dance

You raise the mag up very high
KABOOM, you bring it down
You look underneath the magazine
But, the fly is not around

Goodbye, you putrid little slob
Okay you got away
I'm being cool, not playing the fool
I'll see you again one day

And then the fly said
Buzza boo bop bazink
Which in fly tongue means
"That's what you think."

Daddy By Phone

Once I made a big mistake
Yet, Father God gave me a break
I cheated, yes I even lied
And had a baby on the side
Ulani Colyar is her name
And I'm the only one to blame
Tho' she does not live with me, I'm not alone
I'm still her daddy, daddy by phone

Oh, the baby doesn't live with me
And very little of her do I see
But I love her more than I can say
And think about her everyday
It hurt my wife, it made her sad
But she knows I have to be her dad
The mistake was made by me alone
Still I am her daddy even if just by phone

And I'm determined to teach her things
To try to help her spread her wings
A good life for her I must make
No matter, no matter what it takes,
I wanna teach her so much stuff
She might not let me, but I'll call her bluff
I'll call and call 'til I get her in the zone
Oh, I'm a be her daddy, daddy by phone

Yeah, I wish I could see her everyday
Watch her grow and learn and play
I'm a bug her with love, I won't leave her alone
So, sometimes I'll have to settle for being daddy by phone

And does it hurt a little bit,
You bet it does but I won't quit
I won't quit trying to be her dad
Even if sometimes it makes her mad
And is she pretty, oh boy you bet
The most beautiful girl I ever met
And she's smart and funny and out of the blue
I'm starting to think she likes me too
It's the most wonderful feeling I ever had
The honor of being Ulani's dad
I'll never let her forget she's great
Even tho' she lives in another state
My love for her is bigger than me
I'll teach her a lot, you wait and see
I wanna take her everywhere
I wanna show her how much I care
But until she's ready, I won't change my tone
I'll love her and protect her and be her daddy by phone

5

Fat Folks

Don't laugh, fat folks got feelings too
Stop and think about the things you do
Sure she's healthy, okay, it's true
But that's the reason to make her blue

Don't laugh, fat folks can be hurt too
Why, what the hell's come over you
Just because the man is fat
Gives you no right to laugh like that

Don't laugh, fat folks need respect too
Can't you find nothing better to do
Like washing your face and tying your shoe
Now quit acting like you been out sniffin' glue

Don't laugh, fat folks got feelings too
What if folks decided to laugh at you
Hell, you wear glasses, Mr. McGoo
You've got a face that belongs in the zoo

The kind of breath, I can't speak of
A face that only a mother could love
I hear you're the smartest on your block
With an I.Q. three below a rock

Worst darn breath in the entire south
When you yawn folks try to flip lifesavers into your mouth
You're as coordinated as the average cluck
So ugly you could scare a hungry bulldog off the back of a meat truck

So, don't laugh, fat folks need kindness too
Be nice to them, they'll be nice to you
Don't laugh at folks who are different from you
Or we'll all get together and laugh at you too, Jerk

I Love You

I love you more than apples
Or oranges by the pail
I love you more than haystacks
Or wheat stacked by the bale
I loves you more than Elmer loves
To fix the kitchen sink
I love you, I love you...I think

I love you more than elephants
Altho' I never press
I love you more than fun and games
And that's including chess
I love you more than skating
At the Markman skating rink
I love you, I love you...I think

I love you more than acting
And acting is my life
I love you more than life itself
You'd make a lovely wife
Someday I'm going to smother you
With diamonds, pearls, and mink
Because I love you
I love you
I think

Crack Attack

I was an addict for 23 years (once you are an addict, you always are). So, I'm still an addict, just not a practicing one.

I felt trapped in a coffin made out of my own sense of self-destruction and for what? For an opportunity to blow great relationships, eliminate wonderful opportunities and lose my way...temporarily.

But, now I'm Black...I mean back. I live with the idea that I can change my life at any moment I choose...but which moment shall I choose?

Dope is for losers and hope is for those who have an ability to capture light.

I wrote this to remind my fellow travelers to follow that light, and embrace it.

God is the Greatest High Ever!!!

Crack Attack

You're so smart and oh, so slick
Sucking on that glass stick
Gives you power, for a minute
Then the pipe sucks you up in it
I'm only gonna tell you once more, Jack
You'd better beware of the Crack Attack

Rob your momma, rob your dad
Rip off any friends you've had
Watch your life go from good to bad
It's a Crack Attack

You see, first you start out with just a little
Then somewhere around the middle
That pipe gets as hot as a griddle
It's a Crack Attack

Then, you want a little more
Smoking until your throat gets sore
You're even willing to become a whore
For a little Crack

But then you say, "Not me, not me"
For I control my destiny
Wait a minute, is that a rock I see
No!!!! It isn't Crack

But still you want to check it out
You're looking for a high that will make you shout
You say you want to know what it's all about
Well, it certainly is not about Crack

And so, I leave you with one thought
And some of you won't want to hear it
But the next time you think about checking drugs out
First try checking out your spirit

For you have never known a high
That will make you soar…that will make you fly
Like the intoxicating love from God on high
And when you find that
You will never look back
NO MORE CRACK ATTACK!!!!

Thought 'Bout Ya'

I thought about you last night and I felt warm
T'was like an autumn midst a summer storm
It was refreshing and breathtaking
I found it, at times, making me wonder
Oh, I wondered about your overwhelming charms
And how it would feel being held in your soft arms
Yes, I thought about you last night with a pleasant smile
Thought about you so hard I daydreamed for awhile
I felt your touch, your warm embrace
I kissed your lips, your neck, your face
We lie with bodies wet
From love and tears and sweat
We spoke and laughed and yet
We never said a word
Still, our hearts heard
Oh yeah, I thought about you last night
And I felt good
Felt better than the average man could
I thought about the thrill I feel when
I listen to you talk
I thought about a million things
But the most exciting part
Is reading this poem to you
And sharing the thoughts inside my heart

Oh yeah
I thought about you

RACISM

Racism is a terrible thing. To buy into it is to give up on the light. All types of people contributed to my success, my livelihood, my wellness and my life. My first, non-Black friend was an amazing little old white dude named John Cunnea. He taught me Latin for four years at Morgan Park High School, 1971-1975. He taught me words and their usage, but, he also taught me life lessons and he was my friend.

When I was starting my comedy career, I did stand-up comedy on Venice Beach, California; I was there for nine years (1986-1995). In my first weeks there I was "discovered" by a guy who turned out to be one of my greatest friends, mentors and my godfather. He was a very great help to me in getting started in Hollywood. He believed in me, he loved me. He helped me raise my son, figure out my direction and sponsored my wedding, and he was Jewish… Dan Enright, a pioneer and legend in television and film. He helped me and wanted nothing in return, except to be my friend.

I have been Black all my life and the vast majority of people I grew up knowing are Black. But, others have come into my life and enhanced it in so many ways that I forever turn my back on racism. It's silly; its hurtful and serves no purpose…
Let it go.

Just Because

Just because I was near the scene
Doesn't mean I pulled the trigger
Just because I'm Black
Doesn't mean I'll be your nigger
Just because I'm homeless
It doesn't mean that I'm alone
Just because I'm lonely
Doesn't mean I want to be on my own

Just because I'm Jewish
Doesn't mean that I am cheap
I hope you're not hung up on that trip
'Cause it really ain't that deep
Just because I'm a teenaged mom
Doesn't mean I'm really stupid
Could be I just got sucked in
By some temporary cupid

Just because you're always right
Doesn't mean I'm always wrong
And just because you think I'm weak
It doesn't make you strong

Try not judging me
By all these superficial things
That you are observing
From your pedestal in the wings

That's all
Peace

Why Are Folks in Love with Sex

Why are folks in love with sex?
I'd really like to know
Is it some sort of mystic hex?
Or just a status show?

Is it what makes the world go round?
What life is all about?
Or just a thing that feels so good?
It makes you wanna shout

I've seen a lot of things in life
That make this life complex
But I've never seen anything half as intense
As our deep obsession with sex

I've seen elephants on roller skates
And kangaroos on skis
A polar bear with a boom box
Hippopotami in trees

I once saw a photo of an actual tyrannosaurus rex
But I've never seen anything half as intense as our constant focus on sex

Don't get me wrong y'all
Sex is really good
I've got to have it in my life
Got it every chance I could

But, let's not be in love with sex
Let's love the people instead
So go on out and do your thing
And be careful where you make your bed
(...And play safe)

I've Never Had a Pigeon

Well, I guess I've had most everything in this here wretched life
I've had mumps, measles, gout and old VD
But, of all the things I've had (including Maude, my second wife)
I ain't never had a pigeon shit on me

Well, I know that I've been lagging
And, you think I'm only bragging
But, I'm really givin' thanks, I guarantee
And, good luck has made me happy
You can go ask your pappy
I ain't never had a pigeon shit on me

Well, it happened to my brother
And my sister's cousin's mother
And twice to Billy's landlord, Fred McGee
Happened once to Uncle Jed
And if I'm lying, I'm dead
I ain't never had a pigeon shit on me

So I'm leavin' with the breeze
Can't be standing 'neath these trees
Besides, there's plenty other places I can be
Since I don't like yellow stains
I keep on using my brains
And don't go letting pigeons
Shit on me

Christmas Vampires

As the season rolls around, I mean not to scare
But there is one thing - one terrible thing we must all beware
As chestnuts roast over open fires
Beware my friends of the Christmas vampires

Yes, they're out there my friends
Just look and you will see
And they live for opportunity
They don't care about yo' momma and fuck the homeless too
They really only care about what shit they can take from you

They have no moral compass, their backbones don't exist
And if you aren't paying attention, your ass is on their list
They don't care about holidays, rituals or God
Just show a little vulnerability and that gives them the nod

I saw one rob his momma once, he kicked her down some stairs
And when I said, "That's your momma, boy" He smiled and said, "I don't care"
He said he needs eight dollars, so what else can I say
And I'm going to get in any way I can, plus she's just my stepmother anyway

One Christmas we collected food for the homeless
21 turkeys, 14 hams and a duck
The driver we paid ripped us off for half
And didn't give a fuck

I said, "How could you steal from people in need"
He said, "Why should I care"
So we did what we had to do
We kicked his ass and left him lying there

So at holiday time, please stay alert
Cause if your guard is down, you might get hurt
If you're not looking, you might get snuck
Cause Christmas vampires, don't give a fuck
They will suck you dry to the bone
Especially, if they catch you alone
They're punk ass bastards, they're frail and weak
If they catch you sleepin', they will surely sneak

They'll slip up on you, do a sneak attack
So pay attention and watch your back
And guard your goodies and watch your stuff
Cause being merry is not enough
They'll steal the packages right out of your truck
Cause Christmas vampires really suck

Vanity

I can't help that I'm this fine
It throws me off, it blows my mind
I don't know what it could be
But God just took His time with me

I guess He was feelin' good that day
Explains why He made me look this way
He must have gotten plenty of rest
Cause He wanted me to look the best

He took his time when He made my eyes
And thank God He gave me manly thighs
And I don't want to say ouch
But have y'all seen the size of my pouch

Oh God has been real good to me
Those with eyes can plainly see
And not to make you folks feel small
But God is still workin' on y'all

My Momma Likes Obama

My momma likes Obama and that's alright with me
Some folks said "we need 'the Mitt' if we ever goin' be free"
But my momma likes Obama and that's good enough for me
You can shout it from a mountain, or yell it from a tree
That my momma likes Obama and that's Kool and the Gang to me
My momma likes Obama but here's one point of note
Obama's gonna clear the drama that's why he got my vote
The man makes me believe again that America is great
I'm so excited about the change...my God, I just can't wait
Now the president's not gonna wave a wand
And change everybody's life
He's just a man with a hell of a plan
At least that's what I keep telling my wife
The man is on a mission, and he's gonna make it flow
He's got a plan, let's trust the man
Cause we can't blame it on "the man" no mo'
We're all gonna have to pull our pants up now
Philosophically, if you know what I'm saying
There's work involved, it ain't gonna be easy
And yeah we're gonna have to do a little prayin'
Confidence, faith and patience
Will make the transition complete
But with this team we can realize the dream
And ain't that gonna be sweet

Yeah, my momma likes Obama and hell I love him, too
Cause in my lifetime he's the only cat in that office
That did what he said he would do
And nothing seems to upset him; in crisis he keeps his head
And he's for all the people, did y'all here what I just said

Even tho' the Blair House pulled a dirty trick
Mr. Obama showed his dignity instead of throwing a brick
Even tho' the existing folk keep acting tacky and shady
Mr. Obama is still president and Michelle is still First Lady
Remember when they told Jesus' people there was no room at the inn
His folks preceded to the barn and calmly settled in
Cause like Jesus, his people knew that they had all the power
And in time he would be recognized as he man of the hour
Well ain't nobody calling Obama Jesus and he ain't no Superman
He won't wave a wand and save the world but he'll do the best he can
He comes from a tribe of dignity; I believe his heart it true
My momma likes Obama... and baby, I love him too!

My Mom

My mother transcended on Cinco de Mayo at the ripe young age of 79. She is my rock, my first real fan and my friend. In her latter days, as her health began to decline, she lost focus on some things, but she, always to the end, loved her family, and this dude names Barack Hussein Obama. She brought him to my awareness. One of the greatest joys of her life came on November 4, 2008. Yes, she lived long enough to see our country bring in its first Black president, and if you ask me, the first real, down-to-earth, for-the-people, president, ever.

Oh, the joy in her eyes. I will never forget. And when she passed away, she was wearing a $15, Mr. Barack Obama watch I gave her (with my cheap ass) that she treasured like gold. I love my momma and she loved Mr. Obama. She is my greatest hero. So, Momma, this next one is for you.

Marylena

Marylena is my momma
She's left the room, now stop the drama
Oh her body is not longer in this space
But her beautiful soul is all over the place

I can't be there to mourn with you
For me, she's still alive, I swear it's true
She dances daily in my heart
And we will never be apart

When in your heart a person lies
That person never ever dies
You'll see her in how I treat other folks
She'll flow thru my actions and spice up my jokes

Of all the things I ever did
I'm most proud of being Marylena's kid

My momma taught me many things
That allowed me to spread my wings
She encouraged me to read and look up words
That allows me to soar above the birds

She taught me how to communicate
That gave me a career that's fun and great
When no one else could even see
Marylena believed in me
When no one else came to a show
Marylena was there, don't you know

And so I'll miss hearing her voice
Buying her a hoagie or a smoothie of her choice
Holding her hand and stroking her hair
Little things to remind her that I care

Telling her stories of where I've been
Watching her eyes and enjoying her grin
Cooking her collard greens she thought was nice
I'll even miss her chewing the ice

You'll see her in how I treat others
And how I'll treat my other brothers
And she loved all her sons, it's true
Courtney, Ron and hell, Yoland, too

My momma lived a wonderful life
She loved my kids, she loved my wife
And oh, you should have see her grin
When she saw her man Obama win

Marylena's body ain't here no more
Don't expect her to come walking thru the door
She did all she could around here
Now, it's time to dance and cheer

Yes, Marylena has left the room
But there's no reason for sorrow and gloom
Y'all should celebrate and raise a little hell
Cause Marylena's spirit is alive and well

Don't Lie
For Nicholas

I kissed a leprechaun today
Then wrestled with a bear
I swam across the Nile last night
Then out ran a dozen hare

I told my daddy all of this
He said, "You shouldn't lie,
There's solid proof, always tell the truth
Just like your mommy and I"

I said, "Awright, I'm sorry, dad
I was only making believe
After all the lessons on God I've had
I should know better than to deceive"

But daddy one quick question
(Didn't mean to interrupt your beer)
But where on earth did I come from
And how did I get here

Well he kinda coughed out an "I'm not sure"
Sipped his beer as he spoke with a fetter
"Go ask your mom, my little man,
I'm sure she could tell you better"

"O' Mother, please, I need to know
Where did I come from and why
"You were brought down here," said mother dear
"By a stork like your father and I"
(Sigh)

The Necessary Discipline of Nicholas

My son's name is Nicholas Sebastian Colyar. One of the brightest kids you ever want to meet. Ask him, he'll tell you. Clever beyond his years with all the mischief that accompanies that. I sorta kinda spoiled him a teeny bit. I indulged him greatly; he had all the latest gadgets and toys. Heck, I doted over the kid. But one day, I was having one of those days. You ever have one?

I wasn't in the mood for tolerance…I walked into his room one day and saw the chaos in his room and I went off. But he was just being a kid. I could tell immediately that I went too far. I yelled too much and it didn't teach him…it saddened him. "I'm sorry, Nicholas"…I love you.

Somebody's Gotta Do It
For Nicholas

Don't hate me when I beat my chest
And yell those crazy things
Or when I grow horns on my head
And lose my angelic wings

Don't frown at me when I say no
You can't do this or that
You can't write on the walls today
And please don't bite the cat

I love you more than anyone
Or anything, that's true
That's why I do the things
The way I do the things I do

Don't think I'm mean because I yell
Or spank your little rump
Or when I grit my teeth and sneer
While up and down I jump

Don't think that I'm mistreating you
When I say "No, don't do it"
I'm sorry but the kitty cannot fly
Although you've taped wings to it

I love you more than I could say I'd
give the world to you
But we must do what we feel is best
Cause I'm 24 and you're only 2

And I love you more than anyone Or
anything it's true
That's why I do the things
The way I do the things I do

I love you

31

Seduction

I was riding a bus in Chicago. I sat in the back of the bus, by choice, because Rosa Parks had already done her thang, and I saw this lady get on the bus. She was exciting and sensual but raggedy as a 12-year-old sock...yet, she had something... something in her smile that was so magical, so exciting, that I picked up a discarded brown paper bag from the floor of the bus, borrowed another passenger's pen and wrote this...

Seduction with a Smile

She really didn't look that hot
In fact, good lookin' she was not
Yet she possessed that quality known
As seduction with a smile

No one could claim that she is cute
Most would prefer a substitute
Unless they're caught up helplessly
In her seduction with a smile

She doesn't have long flowin' hair
She doesn't shave her legs with Nair
Still she had the power to make you stare
Seduction with a smile

She doesn't paint her face with dye
She doesn't tint her hair with lye
Yet she could make a grown man cry
Seduction with a smile

She is not given to making scenes
She doesn't wear designer jeans
But she'll teach you what submission means
Seduction with a smile

She doesn't promote lofty airs
She doesn't switch her derriere
But she knows how to make you care
Seduction with a smile

And now I'm standing here dissuaded
All hopes of meeting her have faded
For I have never anticipated
The fact that some other was already sedated
By powers they normally leave you elated
A power which I have already stated
Seduction with a smile

33

Do You Believe in Magic?

Do you believe in magic
I do
I saw a world of magic
When I first laid eyes on you

Do you believe in fairytales
And dreams like I do
I realized how real they are
When I said "hello" to you

And could you possibly believe in romance
I experienced it from our first dance
When I laid eyes on your gentle smile
I knew I'd like your style

I knew from our first touch
That I want you so very much
And as we danced across the floor
More, I wanted you more

And, as we kissed, the fairytale came true
The abracadabras, the shoo-be-doo
The hocus-pocus, the wing of a dove
The kiss was tender, we fell in love

There was the magic rabbit
From out of the blue
Do you, can you believe in magic
I do

Laugh Clown Laugh

Laugh clown laugh
Tho' a mighty load has hit you
And you feel the world has bit you
Where you often have to sit
Laugh clown, laugh
When you feel that love has burned you
And you think your love had turned you
Into something not quite fit

Laugh clown laugh
When the girl you love says screw you
When you thought she really knew you
But she doesn't know at all
Laugh clown laugh
Cause you thought that she believes you
But she walks away and leaves you
And you have to take that fall

Smile clown smile
When you feel that you're a loser
But you really are a chooser
You just haven't chosen them well
Smile clown smile
You should know you're not a sinner
That in fact you are a winner
(But, don't let your big head swell)

Smile fool smile
Tho' the world might seem quite lonely
It's not lonely to you only
And you feel like you can't take it
Be a man and you can make it
Be a man and don't beseech it
Stick your hand out you can reach it
Tho' your tears are tears of passion
Dry your eyes they're not in fashion
Don't you pout and don't be blue
Don't forget that God loves you
Don't forget to stand up tall
Be the biggest man of all
Reach your head up to the sky
Believe you can and you can fly
So you lost at love and song
So what, clown you must stay strong

Laugh clown laugh
Look inside yourself and see
The kind of man you need to be
Reach inside and set him free
And you'll smile
Then you'll throw off all your hurt
Toss your worries in the dirt
And laugh clown laugh, clown laugh

I Simply Couldn't Afford Her

She said she loved me very much
She loved my kiss, she loved my touch
However, she couldn't live on such
I simply couldn't afford her

She said she loved my sexy smile
Tho' she was packing all the while
But, a smile can't finance her lifestyle
I simply couldn't afford her

She said my lips were soft and sweet
My kisses were sweet enough to eat
But cash is by far a sweeter treat
I simply can't afford her

She said my bod was taut and strong
She said my strokes were deep and long
But financial need is her current song
I simply couldn't afford her

She said my eyes were deep and true
She said " You love me and I love you"
"Unfortunately dear, that just won't do"
I simply can't afford her

She said "I'll really miss you, dear"
"It's a matter of economics, I hope that's clear"
And the tears in her eyes said she was sincere
I just simply couldn't afford her

And so we said our last goodbyes
Lumps in our throats, tears in our eyes
And with no regrets, we made our sighs
Too bad, I couldn't afford her

Bye-bye

And Then Came Kellie

The most beautiful girl I've ever seen
I've finally found my ultimate Queen
Golden skin and locs so nappy
I didn't know a brother could be this happy

She's everything my heart desires
In fact, she sets my soul on fire
"Beshert,"I heard my heart roar
For I never have to look anymore

The green eyed girl is Kellie McCann
And I am honored to be her man
And so I thank the God above
For sending me My Perfect Love

About the Author

I enjoy a busy life as an actor, writer, motivational speaker, poet, talk show host and now, author, but really, my bread and butter is telling jokes.

Basically, I am a free-flying comedian who learned his craft on the mean streets of the Southside of Chicago (the projects to be exact, Robert Taylor Homes- not the movie star, the Black architect - 4352 S. State Street Apt. 909, thank you very much).

I always wanted to be in showbiz. I was always heading to California. I woulda made it, too, if my brothers didn't keep bringing me back. Every time things didn't go my way, I would start walking west on 43rd Street because I knew that Hollywood was west from my projects. I just didn't realize it was 3000 miles west. I was a kid. What did I know?

In 1986, I sold everything that wouldn't fit in my 1967 Buick LeSabre, took the cash and drove to L.A. to become a millionaire. But, after discovering that life wasn't about wealth but about finding my true self and loving my brother, I realized that instead of being a millionaire, I wanted to be a billionaire - a billionaire of being. I wanted to be the greatest human I could possibly be. So, instead of trying to make a living, I would live my making and my making shall make my living. Being a great artist and humanitarian is my goal…and I'm gonna have fun doing it.

I discovered Venice Beach and ended up doing comedy on the boardwalk for 9 1/2 years, from 1986 to 1995. Every Saturday and Sunday, I did five 1-hour shows, 40 minutes of telling jokes and 20 minutes of getting my money – fun and finance, yea.

Add to that, over 20 films, including: House Party III, Norbit, Hot Shots Part Deux, The Longshots, multiple television shows, including: Martin, Moesha, Host of BET Live from L.A., HBO Def Comedy Jam, Comic View, Byron Allen's "Comics Unleashed" and the first Black animated Disney feature film, The Princess and the Frog, and, my career is just starting.

I enjoy an amazing life with my beautiful Queen, Kellie, and I have an awesome son and super fabulous daughter, Nicholas and Ulani…in that order. LOL. I believe that everything is about family and God. Once you get Family and God down then everything else takes care of itself.   Thank you, God for blessing me with this awesome adventure…and for having such a great sense of humor. You rock.

Where is Miss Innocent???

From the mouths of babes.
We think we know everything and then we have children and realize we didn't know nothing to start with and even less as we go along.

I've been working on this book for over 20 years...way before my granddaughter, Sian, was even a thought, yet it took her to find, and point out to me the obvious truth that I had completely overlooked. She read the book through and through, heck, she read it three times.
Then she came to me and said, "Pops, where is Miss Innocent?"
I said, "The book is in the next room."
She said, "I read the book... read it three times, but I couldn't find her."
"Find who?" I asked.
"Miss Innocent. The book is called Miss Innocent Goes To Kool Skool...so where is she? Where is Miss Innocent?"

I was stumped by an 11-year-old...couldn't lie to the kid and as mentally quick as she is, I wasn't about to try.

Unless you consider that Miss Innocent is on the cover (which makes her the star and a very big part of the book) or that the stories and the poems are inspired by her outlook on life (which would come off as too metaphysical) or you can just accept my previous explanation in the introduction in the front of the book. Miss Innocent, as a creation, was conceived as an inspiration that developed into a characterization which allows me to partake in this verbal alliteration (I'm probably using this word wrong, but it rhymes).

I don't know what none of that means, but I promise in my next poetry book *Miss Innocent Graduates*, I will have her dance through many of the poems, either in character or spirit, which, if I'm not mistaken, brings us right back to where we started.

Now read this book again. It's tastier the fourth time around.

Namaste

Ivan Artucovich, LA born artist/ illustrator based Valley of Muggio in A.K.A. Ivan Art, is a cartoonist / graphic out of the remote southern Switzerland. Particularly passionate in humorous illustrations, he has been freelancing around the globe for over 25years. Ivan Art first met Michael on the boardwalk of Venice Beach in 1989 when both were street artists.

Ivan Art is active in spreading cannabis awareness as author of Hempathy, food for thought and his Why? Why not? strips are published in various international magazines such as the Italian alternative lifestyle magazine Dolce Vita, Dolce Vita Balkans, the Spanish magazine CannaHabla and the UK publication WeedWorld.

www.ivanart.net
www.why-whynot.net